Fragments of
Her Mind

Fragments of Her Mind

Apaara Kaur

 iUniverse®

FRAGMENTS OF HER MIND

iUniverse books may be ordered through booksellers or by contacting:

iUniverse
1663 Liberty Drive
Bloomington, IN 47403
www.iuniverse.com
844-349-9409

ISBN: 978-1-6632-3361-5 (sc)
ISBN: 978-1-6632-3362-2 (e)

Library of Congress Control Number: 2021925187

Print information available on the last page.

iUniverse rev. date: 01/25/2022

Limitless

My name originates from the fields of Punjab
The Sarovar's cool waters as
It surrounds Amritsar.
My name is a Gurmukhi word,
Found in the Guru Granth Sahib, the holy book of Sikhs.
In English, my name means limitless.
It is boys and men wearing colorful turbans
And the women with their luscious locks that draw people's eyes;
It is the steel bracelet wrapped around my wrist.
It is the Battle of Chamkaur, with Sri Guru Gobind Singh
Leading an army of warriors.
Spears colliding, yells of pain and battle cries.
A fight for our future.
It is the reminder to be courageous like them,
To not succumb to boundaries and injustice.
Limitless.

What's your name? Elementary classmates would always ask;
None could say it correctly.
The teachers were worse.
When the word escaped their lips, my name felt disconnected
and harsh,
As they butchered each syllable into its own word,
Then strung loosely together.

My mother named me
Limitless.
So effortless and gentle,
Yet gripped with confidence and strength.
I want to be limitless.
Shattering the walls of fear and insecurity
That envelop me.
Pulling against an inner voice doubting me.
My name is the never-ending journey.
My name is the freedom to fly wherever I want,
The possibilities, limitless.

Hollywood Actors

We are the true Hollywood actors.
We wake up every morning,
Plaster a smile with pearl white teeth,
Use concealer to hide our acne,
And the dark eyebags from our insomnia.
We change ourselves completely,
Into an entirely new character.
Nobody could ever know about the late nights
Filled with stress and anxiety.
Nobody could ever know the fight
We fight everyday.
This facade, this mask, in it of itself is its own character,
What the world expects us to be.
We walk our own red carpet with such poise
Slowly dying, aching inside,
Acting appears so easy, until you have to do it.
When you have to learn how to change every part of yourself.
But in this mask, we get to be whoever we want,
The world would never know.
But just like anything, soon enough the facade dissipates.
The concealer washes off, and we return to reality.
We no longer portray a character, but our true selves
Yet it is the least desirable role to play.

Masked with a Smile

When did waking up become so difficult
Inexpressible,
This aching I feel
No I'm not invincible
Don't get it twisted,
My mind is a war zone, my body a prison.
As it ruthlessly jails my thoughts and visions,
My vision.
Blurred with tears, trying to blink the flood back, damming in my emotions,
Damn my emotions.
And the sadness I feel,
Who am I to complain and whine, when i have a great deal
That my parents gave me from birth. Privilege.
I don't get to complain!
My problems aren't real,
So I just have to convince my brain,
That I'm fine.
I have family and friends a roof over my head,
I'm sublime.
Screw the mess that is my mind
Muffle the soldiers and their battle cries,
Dry my eyes.
All I have to do is smile.

Lessons from George Floyd

It belongs to Black people to white people and all shades in between.
It belongs to every family who came and dared to dream
But no.
Those shades - they act as a wall.
The difference between freedom for some and freedom for all.
We are just kids, and we see the problem.
Open your eyes, and we can start to solve them.
Trayvon martin, Eric Garner, Breonna Taylor, and George Floyd.
So many others, and yet this conversation we avoid.
Nobody likes facing the hard truth.
But it's necessary, so less kids are stripped from their youth.

No Apologies

This is me without apologies.
The Sikh woman that I am.
Armed with my hair and
A bracelet of steel,
As I proudly walk down a hall.
This is me with no apologies.
Speaking my mind, laughing out loud.
Verbalizing opinionated thoughts
Without a care in the world.
This is me, no apologies.
A nerd in robotics and speech and debate.
Stressing about school and grades.
This is me, no apologies.
With my insecurities, anxiety, and doubt.
Lacking in confidence, drowning in fear.
But I won't say sorry for who I am.
Shutting out the thoughts of others,
Ceasing their whispers.
Because this is me
And I refuse to apologize.

2020

I can't do it anymore
I can't keep it up,
The virus, the pressure,
It is beating me to a pulp.
I know I am blessed.
I know that I'm lucky.
But things are so hard,
Everyone is suffering.
I've become more depressive,
More sad,
More dismissive.
But I can't help it.
This year we swung hard,
And grossly missed it.
Words and numbers
Jumbling up in my head.
I used to be the student,
Now I feel like the teacher instead.
School doesn't make sense.
It feels like the world will end.
And I am just trying to get by
With all my hair on my head.
I've been cooped up for months
No friends, no gatherings.
I am trying to stay positive,
But 2020, you really screwed up everything.

Counting Beats till Death

A mind that is always racing
Not once will it turn off
Stop thinking
Just live.
She succumbs to the heavy breathing,
A lack of air surrounding her.
Finding something to grasp on to
But she's alone.
She fights a battle with her mind
each side armed with thoughts.
Some which want her to live, the others want her to die
She collapses, on the ground,
Not able to walk at this point.
Cheeks soaked in a monsoon of tears.
The only thing calming her is the sound of her heartbeat.
It's so quiet, her mind is exhausted, and all that is present is
the irregular pulsing.
It steadies,
Slowly.
And she counts each beat as her eyes slowly close.
She counts and wonders which beat is her last.
Every beat wanting it to be the last.
But she holds on.

Clings to whatever notion of life she has left.
Living not for herself but for
Who she couldn't bear to see in pain.
So she continues her life,
as if that night didn't exist.
She walks the halls as like any other,
slowly counting the beats until her death.

Do you see me

In your first gaze of me, do you see me?
My hair, the long brown locks that surpass my thighs,
How about my skin color?
"You're taupe" A neighbor once told me.
But only the skin on my face, neck and hands is visible to you.
How about my clothes?
Never a skirt, never a tank-top, never a crop top.
And when you take a second look,
You see my eyes, they're puffy, and my eyelashes are still wet.
You no longer see my cheeks, lips, and nose.
Do you see me?
Or do you see the mask I front.
The one where I explain the swollen eyes are from allergies,
And I wear a sweatshirt in 80 degrees because I'm always so cold.
Do you see past the wall I have built,
The bricks of "I'm fine" stacked atop one another.

In your first gaze, you see my hair,
Will you ever know why it's so long, so beautiful,
Without me having to explain it's Sikh, not "Seek."
Do you see my pride?
Do you see the years of oppression my community, my Khalsa,
have endured?
When I tell you I am a Kaur,
Do you hear my screams of anger as well as the love and joy
I hold for my Sikh brothers and sisters?

Do you see past the words, "I'm fine" and "everything is ok"?
Do you see the girl I became over the course of six months?
No longer innocent, or pure,
Like a white rose that has been stepped on, caked in dirt, and ripped to shreds.
The guilt and insecurities enveloping every thought and moment,
Until they have backed me into a corner I don't know how to escape from.
Do you hear the civil war in my head, the thoughts clashing against each other like swords?
The same battles where I'm no longer fighting to win, but to survive.

The second I turned twelve I stopped wearing skirts, shorts, tank and crop tops.
It would be a crime to show my legs, to unleash them upon the world.

So I ask, do you see me?
Do we see through the physical features and skin-deep beauty?
Do we see past shapes and colors?
Do we hear the civil wars in each other's heads?
Do I see you?

Hair

In sixth grade, I was told my mustache was ugly.
The dark brown locks, no small yet the focal
Point of my entire face.
The hair on my arms earned me the name bigfoot,
They called my mother a gorilla
My body was shameful.
Hairy.
And yet the locks on my head, extending to my thighs
Captured the eyes of envy.
They are exquisite.
Picture-worthy.
Am I beautiful as both Rapunzel and bigfoot?
Am I seen beyond my hair?
Which strands of brown are acceptable?
So you take in the beauty but not the ugly?
You take your scalpel, carving me into pieces,
And shaping me into a picture of your design.
What you'll take and what you'll leave,
What you'll complement and what you'll condemn.
The world does not get to vivisect me.
Like some corpse on a table.

Numb

Why am I numb?
Federal Officers Use Unmarked Vehicles To Grab People In Portland - NPR,
The emotion drained from my body,
Like it is sucked from my soul.
Leaving no feeling from my heart to my toes.
No sadness, or fury, or anything!
Colorado Grocery Store Shooting Leaves 10 Dead - New York Times
This is my world, your world, the world of our generation.
Where the inevitable death is no longer a travesty,
Police ID Suspect And Victims In Shooting Deaths At FedEx Facility In Indianapolis - NPR
But a normal Tuesday.
Nigeria's Police Brutality Crisis: What's Happening Now - New York Times
The world is screaming, tearing itself to shreds,
And I can't feel anything.
American democracy's infrastructure is crumbling- CNN
I can't feel anything.

Somebody, pinch me, pinch me so hard that I feel some sort of pain.

"...a group of pro-Trump militants burst through a flimsy outer barrier on the north-west side of the Capitol building" - The Guardian

Pinch me, so that I can wake up from this awful nightmare, Cause I am sick of being numb.

Damn Magazine

I hate that damn magazine cover.
The one with the slim waist,
Big rear, long hair,
Large bust.
An example of perfection.
I hate that damn magazine cover.
The one that tells me I'm too skinny.
I am not pretty.
I am not worthy of being looked at.
I hate that magazine cover.
The gorgeous girl becomes a skeleton.
She measures her waist, checks the scale,
Counts the calories.
I hate that damn magazine cover.
The "perfect" woman.
I hate that damn magazine cover.
The one society idolizes: unattainable beauty.
Those models are perfect.
But beauty is not skin deep.
Eyeliner doesn't outline your thoughts.
Highlighter doesn't make your dreams shine.
I hate that damn magazine cover.

The United States

Welcome to the United States!
The greatest country on Earth.
Life Liberty and the pursuit of happiness,
Our trio we sought to preserve.
But only if you're white;
Only if you're male;
Only if you're straight, not gay,
And are on the high side of the economic scale.
This country is divided,
Literally left and right.
A polarized nation,
Wanting to start a fight.
Not enough want to listen,
To acknowledge its flaws.
But we're not trying to tear it down,
We're rebuilding it, that's all.
Violence, anti-semitism,
Systemic racism, and hate.
The demons of this country
The bigots we're able to create
It's time we stand together,
Become the United States,
Because when we said all men and women are created equal,
We meant every single race.

I will stand with my country,
Because I still have hope,
Hope that we won't stop fighting
Until marginalized groups get what they're owed
Look at us right now!
We're actually making strides,
And while we're moving forward,
You shouldn't just be satisfied.
And whether or not you voted for him
Biden's the president-elect,
But please, don't get comfortable,
The work hasn't started yet.

Conflicts with God

I grew up reciting mul mantar
The Gurmukhi words fell from my mouth in a recited prayer.
Not knowing what or why.
I grew older, believing if I don't pray every night, or recite
memorized prayers, my wishes wouldn't come true.
If I didn't breathe His name 5 times before every exam, i
wouldn't be granted an A
Because obviously mercy is a bargain.
And love is conditional.
Until I grew up.
I walked in the sun until the shadows consumed me.
The inner anguish, my brain and body on fire.
The insecurities and thoughts of death.
My mind burning into flames.
And when I begged for the pain to stop, for help,
He was nowhere to be found
He, who was supposedly real, and powerful, and gracious.
Was nowhere to be found.
I stopped reciting mul mantar.
Months passed.
I wouldn't breathe His name five times.
I wouldn't breathe His name once.
And all that was left were memories of Him.

Turban

I've grown up around sadhars and sadharnis.
Men and women in my community,
Adorned with head wrappings, ranging in colors across the rainbow.
Heads held high, because their turban is a crown.
A crown that has outlasted years of oppression, sacrifice, faith, and hope.
A crown that has been gifted, from generation to generation.
A crown that tells the world who we are.
Sikhs.
Sons and daughters of a faith, a community, a history.

As a kid, I walked into my parents room,
Watching my father tie his (Turban)
One end of an endless piece of fabric between his teeth,
While he wrapped the cloth around his head.
Other times, he would prep the cloth
Tying it to one end of the doorknob, standing a few feet away,
Tugging at the cloth, trying to straighten it out.
Meanwhile, I ran underneath the line it made
Pretending to play limbo or jump rope.

When I turned eight,
I learned its importance.
Our history, woven into the strands.
But with any crown comes danger.

Our crown is a target.
Met with chants of "*terrorist*!".
Met with fists holding hate.
The perfect scapegoat.

My community is not a danger,
A simple cloth is not a weapon,
And a turban is not a bullseye.

Struggle

Everyday is a struggle.
Every step I take I wish for it to be the last.
I count the hours until I can sleep again,
Because at least sleep helps me avoid what I feel.
I feel different now.
I feel sad, empty, broken.
Walk around my house, hollow.
And you see me.
And yet you don't.
You turn blind to my pain.
As you have done before.
No longer am I vibrant, full of euphoria.
But my mind is screaming, crying, it is never silent.
I am NOT ok.
What once started in my mind spread to my body.
Like vines of agony stretching across
The planes of my arms, torso, and chest
I can't eat.
Every bite is a chore,
But I swallow it, choke it down, no complaints.

The scale remained a countdown, one pound after the next.
I am NOT ok!
Someone! Anyone! Please care. Please notice me.
Be strong enough to ask me if I'm ok,
Because I'm not strong enough to say I'm NOT ok.

Patriotism

I saw the fireworks,
Streaks of blue, pink, green dancing across the sky.
People gazing in awe, their eyes solely focused on the sparks,
Surrounding themselves in a blanket of patriotism.
But our foundation could be delicate like glass.
With an ability to crack.
A frame that only held benefits for those of privilege
Leaving others to fight for the notions of our core values.
A country that was built off fighting for justice and equality.
A nation based on the grounds of protests and riots.
A relentless hope.
And yet, when we fight today, marching
With signs and chants and cries,
For the notions of our core values,
They are drowned out in the name of nationalism.
As if fighting for our rights somehow makes us less American.
The fireworks don't belong to those who silence others.
Who counterprotest for the sake of ignorance.
The fireworks belong to the patriots.
The ones who fight, who hope, who march.
And dream for a better tomorrow.
The ones who care, and realize that
This country is fractured, not shattered,
It cannot be fixed, but improved.

The streaks of blue, pink, and green belong to us.
The ones who fight for others' livelihood.
Challenging the status quo doesn't make us any less American.
I believe it is the very definition of an American.

Torn

Thoughts racing
Zig zagging through her brain
Trying to navigate
The intricate maze.
Infinite walls
Of anxiety,
Self doubt,
And pain
Seems ineradicable.
Something so easy to build,
Is so hard to take down.
Two split selves
Constantly at war
Fighting with
Emotions and thoughts for fists,
Over one question:
Is she good enough?
The words of others
Penetrating her soul.
The walls she built around her
Don't subdue the thoughts of others.
The walls cannot conserve her heart.
Every ounce of love in her is given.
But barely reciprocated.

Soon, there will be no more love.
None to feel, none to give.
The walls so thick,
Leaving none to be received.

You and I

A bond
So sturdy and firm.
Built by love and tears,
laughter and vulnerability,
embraces and kisses,
so durable and strong.
The swords of hate and deceit
couldn't slash it in two.
The arrows of envy and suspicion
couldn't pierce through.
And yet, all it took was us.
A bond that stretched for miles,
as we walked away from one another.
Two different directions.
Two different beings.
Too different.
Love wore thin,
laughter faded,
affection gone.
All that was left was me.
And you were nowhere to be found.
The fire of growth,
The flames engulfed the kindred.
We shared.
All that was left was me.

So permit me
to mourn and grieve.
Standing by the pyre of our past.
Cloaked in white as I watch it fade.
Watch us fade.
A bond burned to ashes
The black flakes of us
scattering the ground.

Ballot

Cast a ballot
As if she is a willing candidate.
As if she seeks your validation
and support.
Vote on her face, her body, her breasts, her ass
As she walks down the street.
Straight face calm eyes,
Not daring to look back.
She is not oblivious to your claims.
She's not naive to your party's beliefs.
Whether or not she is beautiful enough.
Smart enough,
Worthy of your ballot,
That you place into a box with
The rest of society.
Because somehow,
the World believes they
have an Opinion on her.
Marked with your views,
Masked with misogyny,
as if she needs your vote.
Your ballot is dangerous.
It should have never been an election.

Dear Earth

Dear Earth:
Your land ceases to exist,
Water enveloping the solid land.
But the destruction of our home is just a hoax.
Every issue, concern, and threat is repudiated.
But your people shouldn't worry.
Our leaders,
Our knights in shining armor,
Can save this bombsite
Of a world.
But no. The crisis escalates,
They preach to the xenophobic choir
Empty promises,
Fallacious claims,
Stupidity dripping at the end of each and every
Callous words.
Hackneyed chants ringing through the ears of the targeted.
Those whose skin doesn't match the pigment of parchment.
The ones who dare to be brave,
And don't succumb to Americanized stereotypes.
And yet uneducated attentively listen to them.
The beloved leader of the free world which
Holds its arms in shackles.
Their minds filling with hate
As the fog of incompetence and
Misunderstanding, blinds them.

Their eyes are impaired, so one relies on their fingers
To pull a trigger for safety.
But they don't know who they are shooting,
For the naive can't see.
But we can.
This world will someday be bequeathed to me.
This Earth my generation will one day inherit.
And so I don't accept my death.
I refuse to fall into the abyss of madness, because there is hope.
And I am praying for a better tomorrow.
So don't give out on us yet.

Not Okay

I just want some help, make it all be ok
But you say, stop thinking, and it will all go away.
Yet every single day the feeling returns
I am not alright, oh when will you learn.
The bottom of my stomach filled with angst.
Rooted from that one source containing my self hate
I don't trust myself.
I don't love myself.
I hate what I am.
But I am just craving attention aren't I,
So why would anyone give a damn.
I keep opening up and sharing my pain,
But they take my insecurities and use them to their gain.
You see, when you are told something enough times, the words
start to stick.
Soon all you see is the words they pick.
The ugly the awful, they highlight your flaws.
And all you want to do is hide and sob.
And no, this feeling doesn't occur in just a few days,
It grows and grows, like one does with age.
Healing is hard, it needs time,
Unlearning their words is harder,
To ourselves, we must learn to be kind.

HOPE

The things we've heard,
The things we've seen,
Have caused us broken dreams.
The screams and yells,
And shouts and cries
Have landed us with flooded eyes.
The hell and chaos
We have been through,
Has made us not trust you.
The curses and crimes you have told us so,
Will always affect us as we grow.
But we look up to the stars with a knowing smile
Because we understand that this is all worthwhile.
The events that happen in this place,
Will forever leave a small grin plastered
To our face.
We carry on
Throughout the night,
Because you can never
Take our light.
That light is hope,
It fills the air,
And tells us that we will
Not always be in despair.
So here I sleep upon the ground,
Yet I am comfortable for I know
That some light is around.

Printed in the United States
by Baker & Taylor Publisher Services